Henry Stockbridge

The Archives of Maryland

As Illustrating the Spirit of the Times of the Early Colonists

Henry Stockbridge

The Archives of Maryland
As Illustrating the Spirit of the Times of the Early Colonists

ISBN/EAN: 9783337155070

Printed in Europe, USA, Canada, Australia, Japan

Cover: Foto ©ninafisch / pixelio.de

More available books at **www.hansebooks.com**

Fund-Publication, No. 22.

THE
Archives of Maryland

AS ILLUSTRATING

THE SPIRIT OF THE TIMES

OF THE

EARLY COLONISTS.

A Paper read before the Maryland Historical Society,

January 25, 1886,

BY

HENRY STOCKBRIDGE.

Baltimore, 1886.

PEABODY PUBLICATION FUND.

COMMITTEE ON PUBLICATION.

1886.

JOHN W. M. LEE,
BRADLEY T. JOHNSON,
HENRY STOCKBRIDGE.

PRINTED BY JOHN MURPHY & CO.
PRINTERS TO THE MARYLAND HISTORICAL SOCIETY.
BALTIMORE, 1886.

EXPLANATORY.

The following paper was prepared at the request of the Maryland Historical Society, as a sort of codification of the three volumes of Maryland Archives, published for the State by that Society. It makes no claim to original, or extended research, but is confined to the field to which it was limited by the vote of the Society, and has no aim but to alleviate the labor of (or be an index to) the investigation of that publication. The volumes, as issued, are not numbered, and for convenience of reference are cited as if numbered in the order of their publication. This remark is rendered necessary by the fact that the volumes are not in regular succession in point of time, the third volume being synchronous with the other two, giving the Proceedings of the Colonial Council for the same period for which the first and second give the Proceedings of the General Assembly. The first volume issued contained the "Proceedings of the Assembly" from 1637 to 1664, and is referred to as "1 Ar."; the second, "Proceedings of Assembly" from 1666 to 1676, referred to as "2 Ar."; and the third, "Proceedings of the Council" from 1636 to 1667, referred to as "3 Ar."

H. S.

THE "ARCHIVES OF MARYLAND."

WHETHER the "Archives of Maryland" are, or are not books of the sort to which Lord Bacon referred when he wrote, "Some books may be read by deputy, and extracts made of them by others," I trust no apology will be thought necessary for suggesting that they are the sort of books that the average "consumer of modern literature" will be the rather apt to read "by deputy" than in any other way. Possibly it was that thought which induced the Historical Society to request that one be deputized to visit the oases, in what even they regarded as an arid region, and to bring before them a report of the flora and fauna, if any should be found. The Society's mandate to undertake that task is this deputy's excuse for the present paper.

An examination, however, of the three volumes of "Archives of Maryland" now issued is not devoid either of entertainment or profit. The grand old Hebrew prophet called upon his nation for its instruction, "Look unto the rock whence you are hewn, and to the hole of the pit whence ye are digged." In the same spirit it cannot be altogether unwise for us to revert to the beginnings of our civic life, and finding there the germs of many of the customs, institutions, and names that linger with us still—the protoplasm out of which much of the beauty and fragrance of our present social and political life has been evolved—learn their reason and real meaning.

During the thirty years covered by the volume of the Archives which is devoted to the "Proceedings of the Council," and all but a few months of the thirty-eight years covered by the two volumes the "Proceedings of the Assembly," Caecilius Calvert, the second Lord Baltimore, the grantee of the Charter of Maryland, was living, and directing the affairs of the province, as well as it was practicable for him to do from a residence so remote as his in England, with the slow modes of communication then enjoyed, and in a country passing through vicissitudes like those of England at that day. It is a key that unlocks the meaning of many of the events transpiring in the colony, to remember that the period covered by them embraces the last thirteen years of the reign of Charles I. (till 1649), the revolution, chaos, civil war, and Oliver Cromwell's Protectorate of the

Commonwealth for ten years (till 1660), and from that date the restoration, and reign of Charles II.

Under the power granted him in his charter to deputize one to act for him in his absence Lord Baltimore conferred vice-proprietary authority upon persons selected by him, and resident in the province, to exercise there all the high powers with which he was vested—subject at all times, however, to a right of revision and veto still reserved to himself.

This authority was for the most part, conferred upon members of his own family—his brothers Leonard, and Philip, and his "sonne" Charles. The exceptions were that on the death of Leonard Calvert, in 1647, Thomas Greene acted, by deathbed appointment of Leonard, for one year (3 Ar. 187), till William Stone was duly commissioned (Id. 201), and he retained the position, with a brief interruption by the Commissioners of the Council of State for the Commonwealth of England, in 1652 (Id. 271), till supplanted by Commissioners appointed "in the Name of his Highness the Lord Protector of England, Scotland, Ireland and all the dominions thereto belonging" in 1654 (3 Ar. 211). When Lord Baltimore was able to resume his charter rights, in 1656, he was so unfortunate as to select Josias Fendall as his lieutenant; after whose "Mutiny and Sedicōn" he confined himself to his own family—his brother Philip (1660) (3 Ar. 391) and son Charles (1661) (Id. 439).

Lord Baltimore's Authority.

Lord Baltimore's Charter gave him little less than the power of an absolute monarch. It constituted him and his heirs " veros et absolutos dominos et Proprietarios " (3 Ar. 4) of the realm granted him, and thus vested him with all power, civil, military, naval and ecclesiastical—head of Church and State on sea and land. In his exercise and delegation to his lieutenants of the power thus granted he exercised, and delegated all. He never forgets, nor do they, to describe him as "Absolute Lord and Proprietary of the Provinces of Maryland and Avalon," and he is the entire government,—the legislative, the judicial and the executive. Thus his commission to Leonard Calvert " constitutes, ordaines and appoints him our Lieutenant Generall, Admirall, Marshall, Chancellor, Chiefe Justice, Chiefe Magistrate, Chiefe Capt & Comder as well by sea as by land " (3 Ar. 152-3); and when Leonard Calvert was temporarily absent he transferred to " my welbeloved cosin william Brainthw^t Esq." the same offices (Id. 160). The same are embraced in the commission to William Stone (Id. 202-3); and he appointed Thomas Greene, Esq. " to bee his said Lopps Lieveten^{a}nt Generall, Chancellor, Keep of the great Seale, Admirall, chiefe Justice, Magistrate & Comander as well by Sea as by land of this his Lopps Province of

Maryland and the Islands to the same belonging"
(Id. 231, 241). We find the same wide range of
authority and power conferred upon Thomas Hatton (Id. 255), and upon Charles Calvert (Id. 542),
and the Governor and "Councell" contract "Peace
with the Cynicoes Indians" and "make a Warre
wth the Susquahannoughs" (2 Ar. 378), exercising
the highest attribute of sovereignty. The same
power was conferred by the council on Robert
Evelin (Id. 102); on Cornwallis (Id. 133), and on
Fleet (Id. 150). And this was in full harmony
with the claim of Leonard Calvert years before
(1642). On that occasion the Assembly "expressing a great Opposition to the march against certain Indians the Lieu^t General told the Burgesses
he did not intend to advise with them whether
there should be a march or not for that Judgment
belonged solely to himself as appeared by the
Clause of the Patent touching the power of war
and peace, but to see what Assistance they would
Contribute to it in case he should think fit to go"
(1 Ar. 130). The exercise of such high power was
the complaint of the commissioners, Bennett and
Clayborne, who charged that these colonial officials
had pressed against the adherents of the Commonwealth charges of "Sedition & Rebellion
against the Lord Baltemore, whereby not onely
the Lands, houses and plantations of many hundreds of people, but also their Estates and lives

were liable to be taken away at the pleasure of the aforesaid Lord Baltemore and his officers" (Id. 312).

It is true that the charter in giving "free full and absolute Power to Ordain, Make and Enact LAWS" provides that this be done "with the Advice Assent & Approbation of the Freemen of the Province"—but this no more constituted them the legislating power than the requirement at the present day, that certain appointments of the executive shall be subject to confirmation by the senate, constitutes the senate the appointing power. On the contrary, we read of measures discussed and adopted by the assembly and the addition "then the Lieu' General enacted it in his Lordships name for a Law" (1 Ar. 136). Indeed the common form of enactment was "Be it Enacted by the Lord Proprietary with the Assent of the Vpper and Lower howse of the General Assembly" but in the troubled and uncertain times of the English revolution we find them entered "Acts made by William Stone Governor" (1 Ar. 285, 299). Acts passed by the General Assembly and approved by the Governor had force until laid before the Proprietary when his "disassent" rendered them void (1 Ar. 75). It was no uncommon thing for acts passed by the General Assembly to fail of approval by the Governor; and in some instances acts that had passed and met the approval of the Governor were rejected by the Lord Proprietary when examined by him in England. And his dignity and authority were protected by this rigorous enactment.

"All mutinous or sedicious speeches, practices or attempts (without force) tending to divert the obedience of the people from the right Ho[ble] Cecilius nowe Lord Baron of Baltemore, and Lord and Proprietary of this Province or his heirs Lords & Proprietaries of the Province or the Governor of or vnder him or them for the time being (and proved by two sworne witnesses shalbe lyable to bee punished with imprisonm[t] during pleasure, not exceeding one whole yeare, fined, banishm[t] boaring of the Tongue, slitting the nose cutting of one or both Eares, whipping, branding with a redd hot Iron in the hand or forhead, any one or more of these as the Provinciall Court shall thinke fitt."

If such offence was coupled with force, to this assortment of penalties were added—

" losse of hand or the paines of death, confiscacōn of all lands, goods & chattells within the Province banishm[t] ymprisonm[t] during life any one or more of these as the Provinciall Court shall adiudge" (1 Ar. 428).

Meanwhile it required great tact to keep in harmony with the shifting powers of the home government, and, taking one consideration with another, their lot upon the political fence was not a happy one.

The determined effort evidently was to be upon the side of whatever party was dominant in England.

In November, 1649, Greene acting as Governor in the temporary absence of Governor Stone, proclaimed Charles, "the most renowned Prince of Wales the vndoubted rightfull heir to all the dominions of his ffather Charles of blessed memory and Kinge of England Scotland ffrance and Ireland defender of the ffaith &c" and followed this by "a general pardon to all and every the Inhabitants of this Province for all and every Offense and Offenses by them or any of them committed" (3 Ar. 243). In 1654 Governor Stone proclaimed the Commonwealth the government of England and Oliver Cromwell Protector, and granted "a Generall pardon of all offenses Committed in this Province Since the last Generall pardon" (Id. 304). And a Paper in the Public Record Office declares "itt is notoriously knowne that by his express directions his officers and the people there did adhere to the Interests of this Commonwealth when all the other English Plantations" did otherwise (Id. 280). But the English Commonwealth ceased to be and the Stuart dynasty re-ascended the throne, and then, on the nineteenth of November, 1660, the

"Gou' & Councill" "by the speciall order and authority of the Right Honno^{ble} the Lord Proprietary of the Province, Doe according to our duty and allegiance, heartily joyfully and vnanimously acknowledge and proclaime, that imediately upon the decease of our late Soueraigne Lord King Charles the Jmperiall Crowne of the Realme of England and of all the kindoms Dominions and Rights belonging to the same Did by inherent birthright, and lawfull and vndoubted Succession descend and come to his Most Excellent Ma^{ty} Charles the Second as being lineally, iustly and lawfully next heire of the blond Royall of this Realme" (3 Ar. 393).

And yet, five years before, the colonists, by direction of the Proprietary, were so loyal to the existing government as to execute official bonds running to "Oliver Lord Protector of England" (3 Ar. 318).

Land System.

The whole territory described by Lord Baltimore's charter was granted to him absolutely, subject only to the payment to the king of England of two Indian arrows a year, and he was enabled thereby to hold out strong inducements to settlers by proffers of land in large tracts to those who would occupy and improve it. It was not easy however to protect them in the titles granted by him in the manner which was practiced in England, and in 1639 an act was passed rendering enrolment by the Secretary of the Province essential to the perfection of a title by grant from the Lord Proprietary, and another requiring the "Register of every Court to keep a book of Record, in which he shall enter all grants, Conveyances, Titles, and successions to land at the request of any one desiring the same to be entred" (1 Ar. 61, 63).

Voluntary enrolments were much neglected, and the enrolments, made in the Secretary's office under this provision, were "mostly lost or embezzled in the rebellion of 1644," and efforts were made to replace them from the original grants as far as possible (Id. 329; 3 Ar. 230). But the voluntary recording of conveyances, no special sanction being given to the record, proved ineffectual, and in 1671 an act was passed which has undergone very little modification from that day to this, and is substantially our conveyancing, and record system of to-day (2 Ar. 305, 389).

In the "Conditions of Plantations" proclaimed by Lord Baltimore in 1636 (3 Ar. 47), in those of 1642 (Id. 99), and in those of 1648 (Id. 223, 233), liberal grants of land were made to all settlers who chose to avail themselves of them—so much to each man, so much additional for his wife, for each minor child, and for each servant—to be held by the grantee perpetually, yielding specified rents to the Lord Proprietary, thus initiating the unfortunate system of "ground-rents," of the pernicious effects of which we have not yet seen the end.

Special grants of tracts to be "erected into a Mannor," "with such Royalties and Priviledges as are most usually belonging unto Mannors in

Engl^d" were promised and made: Manors of two thousand acres to any person who in any one year transported twenty settlers to the province (3 Ar. 223); manors of three thousand acres to any one who transported thirty persons (Id. 233); while Robert Brooke, for transporting himself, wife, eight sons, two daughters, twenty-one men servants and eight maid servants, was granted one whole county wherever he might see fit to locate, and was made commander and the embodiment of nearly all other offices in such county, as well as a member of the colonial council (3 Ar. 237, 240, 256).

This county was located on the south side of the Patuxent River and called Charles County (3 Ar. 260). But only four years passed before Lord Baltimore lost his abundant love for, and confidence in Robert Brooke, and proceeded to "make Void and Villify" that order and to order that Charles County be absorbed into and make a part of Calvert County (3 Ar. 308).

Among the claims for land under the pledges of Lord Baltimore we find the Jesuit, Thomas Copley, who demanded twenty thousand acres of land for transporting certain persons, twenty in number, into the province, and in his list of persons so transported we find the names, well known to us, of the Jesuit fathers, Mr. Andrew White and Mr. Jo: Altam (3 Ar. 258).

But extensive as was his territory, and lavish as he was in bestowing it upon his subjects, Lord Baltimore apparently had a craving for all the land that joined him, and the gathering of the State's Archives has brought us from the Public Record Office in London, a letter addressed to him by the King as early as July, 1638, rebuking him most sharply for his dealings with the "Planters in the Island near Virginia which they have nominated Kentish Island," warning him to desist and closing with the menacing suggestion, "herein we expect your ready conformity, that we may have no cause of any further mislike" (3 Ar. 78).

But the boundary between Virginia and Maryland on the "Easterne Shore" continued to be a fruitful source of misunderstanding. Oliver Cromwell, in 1653, interposed his authority, as "Captayne Generall of all the forces of the Commonwealth," in most devout phrase, to obtain a "speedy resolution of the question" (3 Ar. 296). Lord Baltimore sent over maps (Id. 319, 327); Commissioners were appointed, and various expedients resorted to, but the question was not resolved in Cromwell's day, as he had hoped.

Upon their other side toward the "Swedish nation inhabiting in Delaware Bay," a conciliatory tone was adopted in order "to worke and preure an Intercourse of trade and Commerce" "which probably may redound much to the benefitt and advantage of this Commonwealth " (Governor Stone, March 1653, 3 Ar. 300).

But when the Dutch planted themselves on the Delaware his Lordship gave "Instruction & Command to send to the Dutch to Command them to be gon." This mission was entrusted to Coll: Nathaniel Vtie of Baltimore County, and he was ordered to

> "make his repaire to the pretended Governor of a People seated in Delaware Bay . . and to require him to depart the Province. . . That in case he find opportunity he insinuate vnto the People there seated that in case they make theyr application to his Lordships Govern^t heere they shall find good Condicōns to all Commers wch shall be made good to them" &c. (3 Ar. 365).

In the negotiations which followed, though there is much to interest and amuse, there is very little of which Marylanders can be proud. The Dutch state their case clearly, logically, and firmly, though mildly, and conclude "Soe wishing the Lord God Allmighty. will Conduct your honno^{rs} both to all prudent results that Wee may liue neighbourly together in this Wilderness to the advancement of Gods Glory and Kingdome of Heaven amongst the Heathens and not to the Destruction of each others Christian bloud whereby to strenigthen the Barbarous Jndians nay rather ioyne in loue and league together against them Which God our Saviour will grant" (3 Ar. 374, 5).

Lord Baltimore blusters, has no name for them but "Ennemies Pyratts & Robbers," orders an expedition against them, "to make Warre against and to pursue said Ennemies Pyratts & Robbers to vanquish & take them And to seize and keep all or any howses and Goods" &c. (Id. 427). But the council deeming discretion the better part of valor, and, apprehending that they could get no assistance from New England or Virginia for the expedition, resolved that "All Attempts be forborne against the said towne of New Amstell & that they finde certainely whether the said towne of New Amstell doe lye within the fortyth degree of Northerly Latidude or not" (Id. 428).

Lord Baltimore was evidently a master of such emphatic epithets and fond of rigorous measures. Captain William Clayborne had all his property of every kind seized for his "sundry insolences Contempts and Rebellions against our lawfull Government and Propriety" (3 Ar. 76, 82, &c.), and was held unpardonable (Id. 205, 221). Ingle is a "rebel," a "pirate" (1 Ar. 238, 270, 301), and a "Notorious and ungrateful villain" (3 Ar. 214, 216), and is exempted from pardon: Gov. Fendall is a "perfideous and perjured fellowe" "a false and vngrateful fellowe" (1 Ar. 420), and is excluded from all pardon (3 Ar. 396). William Fuller is a "violent jncendiary and Seditious 'pson " (3 Ar. 400). John Jenkins and others the same (Id. 445).

While thus jealous of trespasses upon his territory, however, the privileges of settlers which were originally only accorded to English and Irish were extended in 1648 to French, Dutch and Italians (3 Ar. 222, 232), but he excluded from these privileges all "corporations, Societies, Fraternities, Guilds, or Bodies Politick either Spiritual or Temporal," and did not permit any grants that he had made to be assigned to such (3 Ar. 227, 235), "Because all Secrett trusts are usually intended to decieve the Government and State where they are made or some other persons " (Id. 237), and the importation of convicted felons was specially prohibited (2 Ar. 485).

Special encouragement was given to settlers on the Eastern Shore of Virginia to immigrate into the adjoining counties of Maryland (3 Ar. 469, 495), and naturalization was granted to all applicants as a matter of course, as readily as it now is (2 Ar. 144, 205, 271, 282, 330, 400, 403, 460, &c.), without requiring of them that most absurd oath that is now exacted. They merely " promised & engaged to submitt to the Authority of the Right Hon:[ble] Caecilius Lord Baltemore" (3 Ar. 339, 398, 429, 435, 465, 466, 470, 488, 514, 529, 533, 557, &c.).

The Labor System.

Intimately connected of course with the tenure of land was the system of labor, and this, according to the practice in England in that day, was largely servile labor. As already seen, inducements were held out to colonists to transport to the colony as many servants as possible by grants of land proportioned to the number transported. These servants were of two classes—slaves and indentured apprentices, or persons under contract to serve a certain length of time, to repay the cost of their passage from England. In some instances it appears that the length of the period of service was limited by contract entered into before leaving England, and in others was left uncertain, subject to subsequent adjustment. This could not fail to lead to disagreement, and call for legal interposition, and among the laws proposed to the General Assembly of 1638-9, debated and approved, and which failed to become a law, (with all the others then considered) after engrossment, was one " That all persons being Christians (Slaves excepted) of the age of eighteen years or above and brought into this province at the charge and adventure of some other person shall serve such person at whoes charge and adventure they were so transported for the full terme of foure years" and "All persons under the age of eighteen yeeres shall serve until such person shall be of the full age of four and twenty Years" (1 Ar. 80).

Some, however, it is manifest did not submissively render the service which they owed, and in 1641, running away was made felony punishable with death (1 Ar. 107). In 1643 a letter was addressed "to the Governor of the New Netherlands," complaining that "Some servants being lately fledd out of this colony, into yours, we could not but promise o'selves from you that iustice & faire correspondence as to hope that you will remand to vs all such apprentice servants as are or shall run out of this goverm^t in to Yours," &c. (3 Ar. 134). For the purpose of recovering fugitive servants who took refuge among the Indians, an article was inserted in the treaty with the "Jndian Nation of Sasquesahanogh," in July, 1652, which provided that any servant escaping from the one nation and taking refuge with the other "shall with all Convenient speede be retourned back and brought home" (Id. 277). In the same year with the letter to the Governor of the New Netherlands, Lord Baltimore as a matter of economy directed

"That all my carpenters & other apprentice servants be sold forthwith for my best advantage, wch I vnderstand will yield at least 2000^{wt} tob apiece althoughe they have but one yeare to serve, especially if they be carpenters, for I vnderstand that 1500^{wt} of tob is an vsuall rate for the hire of one yeares labour of any ordinary servant. And I conceive it better to hire at a certainty such servants from yeare to yeare as my Commis.rs shall find necessary to looke to my cattell, provide sufficient fodder for them, & to manage my farme at west S.t maries, . . then to have servants apprentices there for that purpose, & to send supplies yearly out of England to them " (3 Ar. 141).

In 1654, and again in 1661, acts were passed prescribing the time which servants should serve those who brought them into the province, grading the time of service from four to seven years, according to the age of the servants, or if they were under twelve years when brought they were not to be free till they reached the age of twenty-one years. These acts required the "masters and owners" of these servants to take them to the Court on their arrival, that the Court might "Judge of their age" and enter the same of record, and to allow them "at the Expiration of their Severall times of Service besides their old Cloathes one Cloth suit one pair of Canvis Drawers, one pair of Shoes & stockings one new Hatt or Capp, one falling Axe one weeding Hoe, two Shirts and three Barrells of Corne " (1 Ar. 352, 409). By the act of 1666 the length of time of serving was increased by one year upon most of the grades of servants (2 Ar. 147). See also Id. 335, 523.

To guard against the loss of slaves by their claiming freedom " according to the lawe of England" as the result of their becoming Christianized and receiving baptism, a law was passed in 1664 that

"all Negroes and other slaues shall serue Durante Vita, And all Children born of any Negro or other slaue be Slaues as their ffathers were for the terme of their liues And forasmuch as divers free borne English women forgettfull of their free Condicōn and to the disgrace of our Nation doe intermarry with Negro Slaues . . . whatsoever free borne woman shall intermarry with any slaue shall Serue the master of such slaue durcing the life of her husband And all the issue of such freeborne woemen soe marryed shall be Slaues as their fathers were" (1 Ar. 526, 533).

But even this act did not sufficiently inspire confidence in the security of this species of property so but what "Severall of the good people of this Prouince were discouraged to import Negroes," and others "to the Great displeasure of Almighty God and the prejudice of the Soules of those poor people Neglected to instruct them in the Christian faith or to Endure or permitt them to Receive the holy Sacrament of Baptisme for the Remission of their Sinns" and it was accordingly enacted in 1671, that "becoming Christian, or receiving the Holy Sacrament of Baptizme"

"the same is not nor shall or ought the same to be denyed adjudged Construed or taken tobe or to amount vnto a manumicōn or freeing Inlarging or discharging any such Negroe or Negroes Slaue or Slaues or any his or their Issue or Issues from his her their or any of their Servitude or Servitudes Bondage or bondages" (2 Ar. 272).

In the revolutionary times of the Commonwealth (1651), an example was set which has been followed in later times, and the power was conferred "to discharge and set free from their masters all such persons soe serving as Soldiers" (3 Ar. 265), as was also another Example by which "all such persons as haue approved themselves faithfull to his Lo^r and don good service were preferred before any others to such places & imployments of trust & profitt as they may be respectively capeable of" (Id. 326).

It was thought necessary in 1666 to enact a law "prohibiting Negros, or any other Seruants to keepe piggs hoggs or any other sort of Swyne, uppon any pretence whatsoeur" (2 Ar. 75), and down to the end of the period covered by these volumes, there was felt to be a necessity for stringent, and yet more stringent laws for preventing the escape of the owned laborers, and securing the return of "Runnawaies" (2 Ar. 146, 298, 523, &c.)

CURRENCY.

The money question was a very serious one with the colonists, and they were forced to devices which would have added lustre to the financial fame of

Lycurgus if he could have hit upon such financial expedients for Sparta. Besides the Indian currency of Peake and Roanoake, which was employed to some extent (3 Ar. 502, 530, 549, 555), Tobacco was a legal tender from the first, though not the exclusive one. In May, 1638, Capt. Henry ffleete gave bond to the government in the penalty of "one hundred pound weight of good beaver" not to trade with any Indians or "transport any truck throughe any part of this Province to trade with any Indians on the South side of Patowmeck River" (1 Ar. 74). In 1640 in collecting his rents Lord Baltimore authorized them to be received in the "Commodities of the Country" and "four pound of tobacco or one peck of wheat" was the equivalent of twelve pence, and two capons equal to "sixteen pound of Tobacco or one Bushel of wheat." Official fees and salaries were rated in tobacco (1 Ar. 57); taxes for ordinary and extraordinary expenses were levied in tobacco (3 Ar. 119, 124); and fines and penalties imposed in tobacco. Governor Charles Calvert (3 Ar. 477), the council (Id. 480), and the General Assembly (2 Ar. 35, 6, 7, 8, 143, &c.), designate tobacco as the "commodity," "the only comodity by which this province doth at present Subsist." But as the supply of this fiat money was practically unlimited, and so became a nuisance, the legislative power required creditors to forbear all collecting of their debts, or accept "Tobacco att the rate of Three halfe pence sterling by the pound of tobacco" (2 Ar. 142, 220). Another measure of relief adopted (1662), was "an acte for Encouragem^t of soweing English Grayne," which provided " that wheate here groweing shall pass and be taken at fine shillings the Bushell: Barley and English pease att three shillings the Bushell, Rye at foure shillings the bushell and oates att two shillings six pence the Bushell " and should be receivable for all debts, public or private, and discount tobacco debts at two pence per pound (1 Ar. 445), and the Lord Proprietary published an ordinance for receiving " dry hydes at two ^{d}p^l and raw hydes at 1^d ½ 'p pound " (3 Ar. 458).

As in mining regions the search for precious metals banishes all ordinary agricultural pursuits, so here the production of tobacco—the substitute for a circulating medium—threatened the colony with starvation. In 1640 a penal act was passed requiring every hand planting tobacco to plant and tend " two acres of Corne," and at the same time another " prohibiting the exportation of Corne "; and the inspection of tobacco, by one of the three viewers who were appointed in every hundred, was made compulsory (1 Ar. 97). These acts or some of them were renewed in 1642 (1 Ar. 160), and repeatedly thereafter (Id. 217, 251, 309, 350, 360, 371; 2 Ar. 561; 3 Ar. 48). But the depreciation of this currency (tobacco), as the result of over production, was so serious an evil, that the colonists made effort after effort for relief, by compelling the suspension of its cultivation (3 Ar. 340, 476, 504, 506, 547). And in 1666 an elaborate non-production treaty was negotiated with Virginia (3 Ar. 550, 558). Lord Baltimore, however, sent from England his " 'Pticular & expresse Disassent, Dissagreement & Disapprobacōn" of the measure and it of course was a nullity (Id. 561). Lord Baltimore tried to furnish a better currency than tobacco by coining money in England and sending it over to the colony (3 Ar. 383, 385); but the Council of State in October, 1659, at the instance of Richard Pight, " Clerk of the Irons in the Mint," "ordered That a Warrant be issued forth for the apprehending of the Lord Baltamore and such others as are suspected be engaged with him in making and transporting money" &c. (Id. 365). Change of administration at home wrought change of condition here, and, in 1661, there was passed "an acte for the Setting vp of a Mint within this Province of Maryland" (1 Ar. 414), and steps were taken to provide bullion for its working and to force its coinage into circulation (Id. 429, 444).

Some idea of the purchasing power of tobacco in exchange for necessaries and luxuries may be formed from the bill presented to the General

Assembly (April 21, 1666), by "John Lawson, High Sheriffe of St. Maries," for executing a negro and two Indians. The items are:

To 2 dayes imprisonm^t the Negro wth dyett	060
To a man to watch him 2 dayes & 1 night	040
To the s^d man for his dyett & paynes	070
To Grane making & other Expences	095
To the Exequuting the s^d 3 persons	800
	1065

but this was deemed an overcharge and he was voted a round thousand pounds in full settlement (2 Ar. 94).

GENERAL ASSEMBLY.

The right of assent or dissent to the laws which Lord Baltimore should propose was conferred upon all the freemen of the province. They were called to meet by proclamation of the Governor and all had a right to participate, but it was promptly provided that the freemen of any locality might meet and "Elect and nominate such and so many persons as they or the maior part of them so assembled shall agree vpon to be the deputies or burgesses for the said freemen in their name and steed to advise and consult of such things as shalbe brought into deliberation in the said assembly" (1 Ar. 74, 154, 259). It was thus a "General Assembly" in fact,—a name that we retain though we have long ceased to know the thing itself.

The Governor exercised the right of requiring by special "Writt" the attendance of anyone not sent as a deputy, and any refusal or neglect to send deputies, or to attend if deputized, or summoned, rendered the "Refusers or Neglecters according to their demerits" liable to a fine, and to be "Declared Enemies to the publick peace of the Province and rebell to the lawful Government thereof" (1 Ar. 328). It was allowable however for any person to be present by proxy instead of in person, and on some occasions the proxies were as numerous as the persons in attendance and some two or three held enough to be a majority of the body.

The assembly when convened was expected to attend to business. At its first meeting the rule adopted was "The house shall sit every day holy days excepted at eight of the Clock in the morning & if any Gentleman or Burgess not appearing upon call at such time as the President is set at or after such hour shall be amerced 20^{lb} of Tobacco to be forthwth paid to the use of the house" (1 Ar. 53), and on the journal at repeated roll calls the entry opposite to names is "Amerced for tardie" (Id. 36, 37, 39), and the amount of the fine for tardiness was, some years later, increased to one hundred pounds (Id. 131), and subsequently reduced to fifty pounds of tobacco (Id. 274). There was also some change in the hour of meeting, special adjournment being made at times to seven o'clock in the morning (2 Ar. 74, 83, 86, 184), never till later than nine. It seems probable, however, that time pieces were not so numerous or accurate as to prevent disputes on the question of tardiness, for in 1642 they adopted this rule, "the drum to beat as near as may be to sun rising and half an hours distance between each beating," and every man who would avoid the fine must be in his place "at the third beating of the drum"—that is one hour after sun rise, and as this was in the month of July, the meeting must have been a little before six o'clock in the morning (1 Ar. 131). That may have been found slightly to interfere with committee work, for the distance between drum beats was, at a subsequent session, changed to one hour (Id. 171).

There was one person in the province who inclined to a very broad interpretation of the term "freemen" as fixing the qualification of persons to sit in the General Assembly. This was Mrs. Margaret Brent, kinswoman of the Calverts, first of her sex here to demand equal rights for women. To the session of 1647-8 she

"came and requested to have vote in the howse for her selfe and voyce allso for that at the last Court 3^d Jan: it was ordered that the said Mrs Brent was to be lookd uppon and received as his Lp^s Attorney. The Gou^r denyed that the s^d Mrs Brent should have any vote in the howse. And the sd Mrs Brent protested agst all proceedings in this pnt Assembly unlesse shee may be pnt. and have vote as aforesd" (1 Ar. 215).

Though the Governor was thus ungallant, and the Lord Proprietary regarded her with anything but favor, the General Assembly appreciated her courage, tact, and ability, in a most perilous time and wrote to his Lordship a year later:

"As for Mrs. Brents undertaking & medling with your Lordships Estate here we do verily Believe and in Conscience report that it was better for the Collonys safety at that time in her hands than in any mans else in the whole Province after your Brothers death for the soldiers would never have treated any other with that Civility and respect and though they were even ready at several times to run into mutiny yet she still pacified them till at the last things were brought to that strait that she must be admitted and declared your Lordships attorney by an order of Court or else all must go to ruin Again and then the second mischief had been doubtless far greater than the former so that . . . we conceive from that time she rather deserved favour from your Honour for her so much Concurring to the publick safety then to be justly liable to all those bitter invectives you have been pleased to express against her" (1 Ar. 239).

In 1650 it was determined that the Assembly "be held by way of vpper & Lower howse to sitt in two distinct roomes apart for the more convenient dispatch of the business to bee consulted of. And th{t} the Gou{r} and Secretary or any one or more of the Counsell for the vpper howse, And any fiue or more of the Burgesses assembled Shall haue the full power of & bee two howses of Assembly to all intents and purposes. And all Bills passed by the s^d two howses shall have the same effect in Law as if they were aduised and assented unto by all the ffreemen of the Province personally " (1 Ar. 272).

That arrangement though then adopted for only the current session still continues. The names by which they appear in the archives are " Upper howse " and " Lower Howse " though the latter in 1675 took to itself the alias name of " House of Commons " (2 Ar. 440). His Lordship retained the prerogative of convening the Assembly when he pleased, and of summoning to sit in it such number as he pleased; but in the time of the Commonwealth, instructed perhaps by events that had transpired in England, it was enacted that the Assembly should be convened at least once in three years (1 Ar. 341), and in 1676 the " Cittizens and deputies of the lower howse of Assembly " complained so loudly to his Lordship because " by his Lordships command fower deputies or delegates had been elected " in each county and then " but two were called by his Lord^{ps} Writt To Sitte in the Assembly " that his Lordship yielded to the request, only exacting an oath of allegiance to himself (2 Ar. 507).

The General Assembly thus constituted, both before and after its division into two houses, shows a purpose to do things decently and in order, and a determination to protect its own prerogatives and dignity. At its first meeting it adopted as a standing rule of order what it often reiterated, till it obtains at the present day—that "no One shall refute another with any nipping or vncivill terms nor shall name another but by some Circumloquation as the Gentlemen or Burgess that spake last or that argued for or against this bill" (1 Ar. 33, 131, 171, 215, 273; 2 Ar. 64, 441). But they apparently found occasion to check something more objectionable than "reuiling speeches," for they adopted the rule that "noe one shall come into eyther of the howses whillst they are sett, with any gun or weapon uppon perill of such fine or censure as the howses shall thinke fitt" (1 Ar. 216, 273; 2 Ar. 65, 441).

The daily sitting would seem to have been terminated at first at the will of the Governor, or Lieutenant General, as the closing entry of the journal each day is "Governor (or Lieutenant General) adjourned the house" (1 Ar. 173, 175, &c.) And though in 1642 "it was declared by the howse that the howse of Assembly may not be adjourn'd or Prorogued but by and with the Consent of the howse" (1 Ar. 117), and a little later there was "the protest of some of the howse against his Lordships power of adjournment"

(1 Ar. 180), his Lordship did not yield the right, and it is only for a short time that we find such entries as "the howse adjourned itself" or "the howse was adjourned by the speaker" (1 Ar. 276, &c.)

Between the two houses a jealousy was soon developed which gave rise to some sharp verbal contentions between them. The one insisted on being regarded as the UPPER House; and the other sturdily maintained an equality, if not superiority. In 1660 it sent "to the Governor and Councell" a message "that this Assembly of Burgesses iudging themselves to be a lawfull Assembly without dependence on any other power in the Province now in being is the highest Court of Judicature. And if any Obiection can be made to the Contrary Wee desire to heare it" (1 Ar. 388). To this communication the upper house gave a somewhat menacing answer "vpon the delivery of wch paper" says its journal "the Burgesses desired a Conference with this Vpper howse by Mr Slye and Mr Thomas Hinson which was Condisended unto." At the conference that followed the Burgesses "intimated that they could not allowe this howse to be a vpper howse" but were willing to "sitt with it as one body." The Governor (Fendall) assented to the arrangement on certain "tearmes" which were so distasteful to the Secretary (Philip Calvert), that he "refused to enter into the lower howse, it being a manifest breach of his Lo[rs] Right Royall Jurisdiction and Seigniory." When they again sat in two houses each appears to have stood stiffly upon its dignity with the other. In 1666 the lower house resent " that their proposals to the Upper Howse for the General Good of this Province upon their Remand from thence hither shall be thus scrible Scrawled & obliterated " (2 Ar. 24), and demand satisfaction for such an offense. A few days later the lower house " desires the upper howse to signify their Assent or Disassent immediately " to a measure it had adopted " for that this howse are resolved to have no further debate thereon " (Id. 37). This was met by a response equally peremptory, and a member was sent to " make known to the Speaker that the Governour expects him with the whole Lower howse in the room where the Upper Howse sitts within half an hour at furthest." The lower house replied that it did not intend by what it had done " to disgust the Upper Howse," and was then soundly lectured and bidden to " take this rule by the Way Obstinate Fortitude is as pernicious to the commonWealth as fearful Honesty " (Id. 42), a proverb that would have done no discredit to Sancho Panza himself. But the upper house could go further than merely lecture the lower in case of disagreement. On the twenty-third of April, 1669, it (consisting of seven members) ordered:

"that the Chancellour & some of the Members of this house go to the Lower House and require them to raze the mutinous & seditious Votes contained in the paper Entituled The Publick Grievances delivered into this House by the Speaker the 20th April last out of their Journall Before which is done this House is Resolved to treat with them no further. It being adjudged in this House that it is an Arraignment of the Lord Proprietor the Governor & Council " (2 Ar. 177).

For the four succeeding days the two august bodies maintained a most pugnacious attitude. The upper house imperiously demanded an expurgation of the journal of the lower house; and the lower gave reason and rhetoric for its refusal. It said:

" We are sorry exceeding Sorry that We are driven to Say that your Answer & Objections to the paper Entituled the Publick Grievances are not Satisfactory or that by the refulgent Lustre of the Eradiations of Reason that shine & dart from them the weak & dim Eye of our Understandings is dazled & struck into Obscurity . . . We shall be willing to have our Journal Contradicted, expunged, obliterated, burnt, anything, and to have our Grievances appear in any form or dress of words most pleasing to yourselves if We might be assured that the Weight and pressure of them vnder which the Country groans & cryes might be removed " (Id. 180).

The obnoxious entry was in the end compromisingly removed, though the " Grievances " were but partially so.

The vigilance with which both houses guarded their dignity and punished " Contempt " and the latitude given to the definition of "Contempt" spared neither bar-room nor pulpit. Upon the journal of the upper house is entered, " then came a Member from the Lower House to desire leave to Speak with Col. Wm. Evans being a Member of this House which was granted " (2 Ar. 14).

Mr. James Browne " being Elected as one of the Deputies & Delegates of Baltimore County " did not " attend his service of the Country in the General Assembly," and it was " ordered thereupon that the said James Browne be for his Contempt af^d fined forty pounds Sterling " (2 Ar. 243).

If the absence of the member was involuntary it would seem that the absentee was subjected to no punishment except the loss of pay and perquisites; for at the end of the session of 1650, when the committee brought in their " bill of charges " and allowed each member fifty pounds of tobacco for each day's attendance they report " As for that M^r ffrancis Brooks was not able through sickness to attend the howse, and drawing of his wine the Committee thinke fitt, not to provide for him att all " (1 Ar. 284).

But when the person supposed to be guilty of contempt was within reach he did not escape with a mere fine. James Lewis " had abused Mr. Vanhacke one of the members of the Lower House " and for this contempt the upper house " Ordered that the said James Lewis go into the Lower House and upon his Knees ask the whole House forgiveness and Mr. Vanhacke in particular and pay for a fine 2000 lb tob°" (Id. 254).

More grievous still was the contempt, and the punishment of "Edward Erbury Merchant of the Sare of Bristoll," against whom it was alleged (May first, 1666):

"there was an abuse Comitted last night to the disturbance of the whole howse in their quiett & rest. And the s^d Erbury did call the whole howse Papists, Rogues, ——Rogues" . . . "and there is not one in the Cuntry deserves to keepe me Company;" . . . "and vpon a full debate thereon had in this howse, They doe judge the same to be a scandall to the Lord Prop^r to his Lieutenn^t Generall & to both howses of Assembly & a greate Refleccōn upon the whole Province in Generall And therefore vnanimously voted by this howse that the s^d Erbury be brought before this howse to giue answere to the abovesaid Charge in relacōn to those Informacōns now giuen in ag^t him."

And he was accordingly brought before the house and being

"taxed by the speaker of all those words spoken . . . . he answered that he remembered none of those words as is alledged Only he Confesseth that he was in drinke and remembers not that ever he spoke such words. Which answere being taken into Consideracōn the howse doe judge the same altogether vnsattisfactory & th^t noe 'pson of full age shall take advantage by drunkennes in such case."

And the lower house upon this conviction referred the case to the upper house to prescribe fit punishment for the grave offense, and

"the vpper howse doe order that the s^d Erbury be tyed to the Aple tree before the howse of Assembly & be there publickly whipt vpon the bare back with thirty-nine lashes . . . & that the s^d Erbury doe pay the sheriff his fees. . . . And further ordered that the s^d Erbury be after he is whipt brought into both howses of Assembly publickly to aske them forgiueness" (2 Ar. 55, 120).

On Wednesday, April fourteenth, 1669, Charles Nicholett preached a sermon before the lower house in which he exhorted them to " Beware of that sin of permission," and " to goe on with Courage " to discharge their duties " agreeable to their own Conscience," and it being thereupon charged in the upper house " that Charles Nicholett hath spoken seditious Words against the Government of the Province, It is ordered that a Messenger be dispatched away to fetch the said Nicholett to make his Appearance in this House to abide the Censure of the House for the said Seditious Speeches " (Id. 159). His explanation when he appeared, though not the same as Erbury's was no more satisfactory than his had been, and it was thereupon:

"Ordered that the said Nicholett go to the Lower House & there acknowledge his Error in his late Sermon preached to the Lower House in that he medled with Businesses relating merely to the Government & there to crave the pardon of the Lord Proprietor the Lieutenant General & the Assembly & that he bring the Certificate under the hand of the Clerk that he has done it in the face of the whole House . . . and that he pay unto John Gittings Clerk of the Assembly forty shillings or the value thereof in Tobacco for Fees."

This order was "returned from the lower house underneath which was written, Mr. Nicholett acknowledged in the Lower House as is above written " (Id. 163).

They appear to have been as averse to dishonesty among themselves as to political preaching by their ministers, for in the session of 1676 they enacted a fine of four thousand pounds of tobacco against Henry Ward of "Caecil County:"

"for that being a member of the last Assembly he did Informe the said lower house that he had a very good horse lost in the Conntry service in the expedicōn to the Whorekills And that the Lower house giveing creditt to such Informacōn did thinke fitt to allow him out of the Publick Leavy Eighteene hundred pounds of tobacco, And it is now made Evidently appeare that the said Ward lost noe such horse in the Publick service and that the said allegacōn was most egregiously false " (2 Ar. 540).

His fine was thus a little more than twice the amount of his dishonest gain.

Penal Law.

This idea of restitution to the injured pervades many of the acts both of the General Assembly, and of the Council. Thus a servant running away was held to a double term of service (1 Ar. 348); and one harboring the runaway was responsible for all damages sustained by the escape (Id. 451). Whosoever should "wrongfully kill or carry away any marked swyne of another man's must pay double the value of such swyne to the true owner thereof, and 200^l of Tob. more to him that shall inform thereof, and 300^l of Tob. more for a ffine to the Lord Prop^r" (1 Ar. 251; 2 Ar. 29). This was afterwards increased to treble the value of the hogs stolen (2 Ar. 278). Again it was enacted, (1654) that "whosoever shall take and Carry away any of the Goods or Chattels of any person contrary to the owners will shall restore four fould if able and if not the person or persons so offending as aforesaid shall make the said four fould satisfaction by servitude" (1 Ar. 344).

The same principle rules in several laws which provide that a man who has incurred a debt without the means to pay it should make restitution by personal service—in other words, should work it out (1 Ar. 70, 152, 188). And, as a security for the creditor, no debtor might have a pass, without which he could not leave the county of his residence (Id. 160, 174, 194).

The same principle was applied to "letigeous persons" by providing that "all persons whatsoever that are Cast in any cause be they p.^{lf} or def^{te} shall be amerced (besides the damages and Cost to the Recoverour) flifty pounds of Tobacco" (1 Ar. 486).

This was milder than the Council desired, for its recommendation was "that the party cast in appeale shall pay treble dammages for the prevention of vexatious sutes" (3 Ar. 341).

Perhaps the most severe application of this principle was in the provision that "if the Judge thinke any verdict greivious to either party . . . and the jury evidently partiall or willfull he may charge another jury to enquire and try by the same evidence, and if they find contrary to the former jury all the former jury may be fined at the discretion of the Judge" (1 Ar. 152).

It is probable that under this law the office of a juror became as unpopular as was the office of a constable in New York under the administration of Wouter Van Twiller. It must not be thought, however, that the Government provided no punishment for crime but restitution to the injured. On the contrary it seems to have had quite a penchant for imposing "Condigne punishm^t" upon a wrong doer "that Soe he may be a Tirrable Example To others of Offending" (2 Ar. 491). In the session of 1638-9 there was passed to the point of engrossment "an act Determining Enormious Offenses" (1 Ar. 73), designed no doubt to give a catalogue and definition of the acts which should be treated as felony and render the offender infamous. By repeated acts it was provided that the "Inhabitants of this Province shall have all their rights and liberties according to the great charter of England" (1 Ar. 83), and nothing should "in any sorte infringe or prejudice the Just and lawfull Lybertyes or priviledges of the free borne subjects of the Kingdome of England" (1 Ar. 300, 398), and that justice should have no delay was embodied in the oath of the Lieutenant General, Councillors and other officers (3 Ar. 210, 213), and in matters where there had been no special enactment for the Province, there "right & just shall be determined according to equity & good concience not neglecting (so far as the Judge or Judges shall be informed thereof & shall find no inconvenience in applycation to this Province) the rules by which right & just useth and ought to be determined in England in the same or like cases" (1 Ar. 147, 183-4, 435, 448, 487, 504, &c.)

The large discretion given to the Judge in that law was confided to the Judge, Governor or Lieutenant General by repeated acts, and the punishment of many offenses (counterfeiting for example) was left entirely at the discretion of the Governor (1 Ar. 247). Perhaps this was unavoidable in the paucity of prisons, or means of restraint; but there were some offenses which the General Assembly determined so far as they were concerned should not by any possibility, be committed twice by the same person; and others which they wished should bear a sure punishment which all should understand could not be tempered by judicial leniency. Treason to the king. the Lord Proprietary, or the Lieutenant General, they made punishable by drawing, hanging and quartering of a man; by drawing and burning of a woman, corruption of blood and forfeiture of all property and franchises: Petit treason was to be punished by drawing and hanging of a man, by burning of a woman; sorcery, blasphemy and idolatry by burning; "Burglary, Robbery, Polygamie, Sacriledge, Sodomy and Rape" by hanging. The exceptions to these modes of punishment in this bill were two, to wit: "the punishment of death shall be inflicted on a Lord of a Mannour by beheading . . . and if the offender can read Clerklike in the judgment of the Court then the offender shall lose his hand or be burned in the hand or forehead with a hot iron & forfeit all his lands: againe offending he shall for such second offense suffer pains of death & forfeit all lands and goods and Chattells" (1 Ar. 71-2).

In 1641, and again in 1642, it was published under the Greate Scale that "It shall be felony in any apprentice servant to depart away from his or her master or dame with intent to convey him or her selfe out of the Province," and in any other person to "Accompany such servant in such unlawfull departure. And the offenders therein shall suffer paines of death" (1 Ar. 107, 124).

In 1650, "Everyone giving false witnes vppon oath or perswading or hiring another to give such false witnes vppon oath shalbe nayled to the Pillory and loose both Eares or put to other corporall shame or correccōn as the Court shall Adiudge:" For striking an officer, or witness, or any other person in presence of the Court, the offender was to lose his hand (1 Ar. 286, 350).

"If any Idle and Buss-headed person" forged and divulged "false rumors news and reports, or by Slandering tale bearing or back biting Scandalized the Good Name of any person" he was doomed to pay "from 1000 to 2000 pounds of tobacco and be Censured by way of Satisfaction to the Party Injured thereby" (1 Ar. 343; 2 Ar. 273).

In 1663 it was enacted "Th^t a Pillory & Stocks bee sett vpp att every Co^{rt} howse in Each respective County & a Ducking Stoole in the most convenient place of the County," and "th^t the Com^r of each County Co^{rt} provide an iron for the burning of Malefactors wth the L^{r}e R. & anoth^r wth the L^{r}e H." (1 Ar. 490, 491). But for St. Mary's as the metropolitan County, an additional luxury was provided at the same time in the enactment "th^t a

Logg howse be built Twenty foot square at St. Mary's vppon the Counteyes lands for a Prison" (1 Ar. 490), at an expense of two thousand pounds of tobacco. Whether the officials were blind to their duties and privileges does not clearly appear ; but three years later a law was published under the Great Seal of the Province for something more pretentious—" that there be foure acres of land neerest about the Spring on the East side of St. Maries feild be allotted to build a prison vpon and that there be tenn thousand pounds of tob. raysed out of the province to be laid out in building the prison" (2 Ar. 139). This prison was intended for the accommodation of debtors as well as criminals (Ibid. and Id. 542).

It was probably on account of the inconvenience of having but one place of detention for the whole province, and not local jealousy on the part of the County, that led to the enactment three years later " that there be a Logg house Prison Twenty ffoot square Built at Augustine Harman's in Baltymore County at an expense of tenn thousand pounds of tobacco for p'venting servants & Criminall 'psons from Running out of this Province" (2 Ar. 224).

In what part of the County Augustine Harman's was does not appear. but the commissioners of the County could not agree as to the location of the Court House, and the upper house of the Assembly, after waiting four years, decided for them, in

February, 1675, that "the most Convenient Place for the same will be the head of Gunpowder River on the North Side," and ordered it erected there accordingly (2 Ar. 430). Probably the desire to have a locality that was accessible to that part of the County that was on the "Easterne side of the bay" (3 Ar. 530), had its influence in determining the selection.

The Indian Question.

It is due to the truth of history, though it may not be flattering to pride of ancestry, to say that these volumes show that the Indians were always under suspicion, and had few rights which the colonists considered themselves bound to respect; that in fact they sympathized deeply with the feeling that is said to have induced another set of men to resolve; (1) "The earth hath the Lord given to his saints, and (2) Resolved that we are his saints." The colonists do not appear to have been ever troubled with a doubt of the power and right of King Charles to give all lands and waters absolutely to Lord Baltimore, or of Lord Baltimore to grant it on such conditions as he pleased to them; and in this firm belief they regarded vessels which came to their shores without his or their permission as pirates, and all persons presuming to place foot thereon without recognizing their allegiance to Lord Baltimore, whether Dutch, Swedes, or Indians, as intruders, trespassers, public enemies.

An illustration of this is furnished in the case of "a Certaine Ship called the Maid of Gaunt in 1654." This ship had traded in Virginia by warrant of the Governor of that province, and came into St. George's River apparently on the same peaceful errand. At all events she had shipped part of a cargo belonging to Marylanders, but upon the allegation that "the owner and Merchants thereof were Inhabitants of the King of Spain's Dominion" "Cap' Thomas Webber master of the Good Ship Called the Mayflower of London" "with the assistance of said ship, men and Ammunition" captured her, held her as prize, and was sustained therein by Governor Stone (3 Ar. 297, 305).

As early as May, 1638, the council coneeiving that "in so remote an Iland as the Ile of Kent and situate among divers Salvage nations, the incursions as well of the Salvages as of other enemies pyrates and robbers may probably be feared" appointed John Boteler "Captaine of the military band of that Ile of Kent in all martiall matters" with "full power to leavie muster and traine all sorts of men able to beare arms and in case of any sodaine invasions of Salvages or Pyrates to make warre and to vse all necessary meanes to the resistance and vanquishing of the enemy" (3 Ar. 75).

Among the acts engrossed for a third reading in March, 1639, but laid over with all the others was one that required every housekeeper to have at all times in his or her house for every person "able to beare armes one Serviceable fixed gunne of bastard muskett boare one pair of bandaleers or shott bagg one pound of good powder foure pound of pistol or muskett shott and Sufficient quantity of match for match locks and of flint for fire locks" (1 Ar. 77).

In January, 1639, Governor Leonard Calvert, because that "Certain Indians of the Nation called the Maquantequats have Comitted Sundry Insolences and rapines upon the English inhabiting within this Province" and refused the satisfaction that was demanded "and therefore Compelled us to enforce them thereunto by the Justice of a warr" commissioned Nicholas Harvey to go "with any Company of English as Shall be willing to goe along sufficiently provided of arms to invade the said Mancantequuts and against them and their Lands and goods to execute and Inflict what may be inflicted by the Law of warr and the pillage and booty therein gotton to part and divide among the Company that Shall performe the Service" (3 Ar. 87). Similar declarations of war, or commissions for military service, against the "Sesquihanowes," or other aborigines were issued year after year, and sometimes two and three times in a year, and though the reason assigned at times is "Satisfaction for Outrages" it is quite as often "punishing insolences," or preventing them, and the officer is commissioned "to goe out upon said Ind: or aid: confeder: as shalbe found in any suspicious manner & them to expell or vanquish & putt to death, & their armes or goods to pillage, & thereof to dispose at yor discretion, & to destroy them or any other misch: doe vnto them by law war" (3 Ar. 132, 137, &c.)

The proceedings had not always the pretence of following the laws of war. In 1641 Governor Leonard Calvert proclaimed " I do hereby authorize and declare it lawfull to any Inhabitant whatsoever of the isle of Kent to Shoot wound or kill any Indian whatsoever comeing upon the said island" (3 Ar. 99). But the colonists of Kent Island were not long to enjoy a monopoly of this amusement. The next year his proclamation was, " I doe hereby authorize all or any of the English of this Colony to shoote or kell any Indian or Indians in any part about patuxent river that shalbe scene or mett either vpon the land or water without the said bound after sixe daies after the date hereof, except such as have or bear visibly a white flag or fane" (3 Ar. 126, 147). With such measures of defense and protection it is little wonder that we find it proclaimed a few months later "these are to publish & declare that the Sesquihanowes Wicomeses, and Nantacoque Indians are enemies of this province, and as such are to be reputed & proceeded against by all persons" (Id. 116, 118), or "noe man able to bear arms shall go to church or Chappell or any considerable distance from home without fixed gunn and 1 charge at least of powder and shott" (Id. 103, see also 1 Ar. 254).

The cattle of the colonists, unrestrained, drew no nice distinctions between the crops of their owners and those of the Indians, and their hogs running at large seem to have been a novel and attractive species of game for the Indians, who could not understand why they should not protect their own crops, and hunt all animals running in the woods, as for generations they had been accustomed to do. For redress the person who had suffered "Spoil in his Swine" was permitted to demand "satisfaction of any town whose Indians have done him such spoil;" and, in case of refusal, or delay to comply with the demand, had "free Liberty to right himself upon any the persons or Goods belonging to that Town by all means that he may" (3 Ar. 96). With this free license for reprisals it was by no means desirable that the barbarians should have civilized weapons, and so an act of the General Assembly to prevent this was passed (1648) that "noe Inhabitant of this Province shall deliver any Gunn or Ammunition to any Pagan" (1 Ar. 233); changed in form the next year to "Noe Inhabitant of this Province shall deliver any Gunne or

Gunnes or Amunicōn or other kind of Martiall Armes to any Indian borne of Indian parentage" (Id. 250).

The Governor and Council earnestly sustained this policy of disarmament (3 Ar. 144, 160, 260); and yet it did not secure satisfactory exemption from "Insolences." The Indians even had the assurance in 1666 to appear before the General Assembly and demand that one rule should be applied to both peoples. They complained:

"Your hogs & Cattle injure Us. You come too near us to live and drive Us from place to place. We can fly no further let us know where to live & how to be secured for the future from the Hogs & Cattle. Emerson hath thrown down the fence made by the Indians at Nanjimy about their corn by which eight men have lost their whole Crop of Corn for which they Complain & desire to be secured for the future. Let us have no Quarrels for Killing Hogs no more than for the Cows Eating the Indians Corn. If an Indian kill an English let him be delivered up Mrs Langsworth's children were killed and the Murtherers were delivered they found a Man Indian dead in the path killed by the English for which thay have no Satisfaction & desire it may be Considered" (2 Ar. 15).

The summary manner in which such "murtherers" were disposed of when so delivered up is illustrated by an entry in the journal of the Assembly two years later when the Lieutenant General sent it the following message:

"You have here sent you the Indian that murdered Capt. Odber it is that Rogue that caused our late Troubles Ababcos Indians have brought him Mr Henry Coursey knows the Indian & does assure me that this is the Fellow that shott the said Odber I do hereby order that this Murderer be executed at St. Mary's toMorrow."

But the General Assembly could not tolerate such procrastination and indulgence but "Ordered that the said Wianamon be shott to death here at St. Mary's some time before three of the Clock this Afternoon" (2 Ar. 195).

The methods adopted for protection did not differ materially from those still in vogue whereever the two races come in contact:—expeditions against them,—confining them to reservations,—binding them by treaty.

The first regular expedition against them was authorized in 1642 when it was enacted that "It shalbe lawfull to the Lieutenant Generall to make an expedition ags^t the Sesquihanoughs or other Indians as have committed the late outrages vpon the English at such time & in such manner as he shall think fitt" (1 Ar. 196, 8, &c.). In 1643 Capt. Tho Cornwaleys Esq having a "propensenes to goe a march vpon the Sesquihanowes" was authorised "for the vindication of the honour of God, & the Xtian and the English name vpon those barbarians & inhumane pagans" "to levie volunteers & to doe all other things requisite for the training of the souldiers punishing of insolences vanquishing the enemies and disposing of the spoiles" (3 Ar. 133). In 1644 Capt. Henry fflecte was commissioned " to goe vp wth yor company to pascatoway and there to consider whether it willbe more to the honor, safety, or advantage of the English to have war or truce wth the Sesquihanowes at this present," and if he " shall not think best to treate or truce wth them you are to vse all lawfull & discreet meanes you can to pillage or take them or if it shall seeme best to kill them; and to break off all league and treaty betweene them and our confederates" (Id. 149, 150).

In 1647 because that " sundry the inhab^{ts} of this province had sustayned diuers great losses in their estates by the Indians of Nantacoke & Wicomick" Captain John Price was commissioned " to take 30 or 40 such able men as he shall thinke fitt and make choyce of" and go to the Eastern Shore and there to " imploy his uttmost endeauor skill & force by what meanes hee may, in destroying the s^d Nations, as well by land as by water, eyther by killing them, taking them prisoners burning their howses destroying their Corne, or by any other meanes as he shall iudge convenient" (3 Ar. 191).

In 1652, in an expedition ordered against the " Easterne shore Indians" at the instance of the " inhabitants of the Isle of Kent" for the " Suppressing of those heathens and avenging of Guiltless Bloud and the preservation of our lives with our wives and children" (Id. 279) it was "ordered by the Council that for all Such Indian prisoners as Shall happē to be taken and brought in when this March is ended they shall be divided according to their Valuation upon a Generall Division throughout the Province amongst" those who had defrayed the expenses of the expedition (Id. 283-4), but that it was not intended that this enslaving of the Indians should extend beyond those whom they were pleased to consider enemies is manifest from an act of Assembly passed in 1654, enacting that "whatsoever person or persons that shall steale any friend Indian or Indians whatsoever or be accessory in Stealing them and shall sell him or them or transport them out of the County shall be punished with death" (1 Ar. 346).

Twenty years later these "friend Indians" rendered the colony such service that it was "Voted by the house th^t Matchcoats Corne Powder and Shott be purchased and forthwith delivered to the friend Indians by way of gratification for the Services done by the Said Indians in the late Warre ag^t the Susquehannough Indians, viz to the Puscutaway, Chapticoe, Nangemy, Mattawoman & Pamunkie Indians" (2 Ar. 488). Yet such was the distrust of everything bearing the name of Indian, that this same vote, that gave this substantial recognition of favors received from them, required them to deliver hostages to the English.

Although the proposition that "the only good Indian is a dead Indian" had not then been enunciated, yet the germ of that sentiment was clearly vital among them. Tho Matthews, with his brother Ignatius, and Henry More, in 1664, went by invitation to an entertainment given by the "Indeans of Pascataway" who "had taken two prisoners of the Johnadoes upon the North side of patomake river" and reported to Governor Charles Calvert "After I came they presently began to torter the man and gave mee this Relacōn . . . as for the Relacōn & maner of their tortering th^m I omitt till I shall see yor hono^r" (3 Ar. 501).

Though they may have been interested spectators when one tribe of Indians tortured another I find in the Archives no evidence that they themselves resorted to torture to obtain information— at least they did not when they thought a different course more certain of obtaining it (Id. 493); still, when they went to war, they meant war and not peace; and on the same date as the last occurrence the Council "Ordered th^t Warr be pclaimed ag^t the Cinego Indians th^t a Reward of a hundred Armes lenght of RoanOake be giuen to eury 'pson whether Indian or English th^t shall bring in a Cinego prison^r or both his Eares if he be slayne" (Id. 502), and at the same time it was declared "to be lawfull for any 'pson Inhabiting in this prouince to kill slay or take prisoner any of the aforesaid

Cinego or Johnado Indians that shall enter this prouince" (Id. 503). But the saddest illustration of their manner of dealing with the Indians, in what they called war, which is presented in these volumes, is found in the pages that record the events of the expedition under the command of Thomas Truman against the Susquehanna Indians in 1676. These Indians, though a very powerful tribe, had shown themselves desirous of peace with the colonists, and it is proof of their favorable inclination that when a treaty was negotiated with them, the reason assigned in the Council was, because that "the Indians had a long time desired and much pressed for the conclusion of a peace with the Government and Inhabitants of this Province which as is now conceived may tend very much to the Safety & advantage of the Inhabitants here if advisedly effected" (3 Ar. 276); and, for the same reason doubtless, a further alliance offensive and defensive was made with them in 1661 (Id. 420), and yet a further one in 1666 (Id. 549), and in this last year the general Assembly had declared that the "honor of his Lordship and the English Nacōn will vndoubtedly suffer by breach of faith even to a Heathen" (2 Ar. 131), but the officers of this expedition forgot so just a sentiment.

The plain facts of this transaction seem to be that, in 1675, the Susquehanna Indians, being harassed by the Senecas, as they had often been before, came to the English settlements, and asked for permission to live among the "friend Indians" near the settlements; and this privilege being refused them they "did condescend to remove as farr as the head of the Potowmack" (2 Ar. 429-30). Later in the season there were depredations committed upon the settlers in Baltimore and Anne Arundel Counties, and also in Virginia, and a joint expedition into the Indian country was fitted out by the two colonies under the command of Thomas Truman. He, with his force, appeared "At the forte of the Susquehannoughs . . . on the North side of Puscattuway Creek . . . on the Sabboth morning about the 25 or 26 day of September" . . . and sent a messenger to the fort and desired "some of their great men to come and Speake with the s^d Majo^r vpon which message of his there came out 3 or 4 of them;" afterwards thirty or forty. They were told "of the great jnjuries that had been done to the Country and th^t he came to know who they were th^t had done them, And the great men Replyed that it was the Seneeaes." Further parley ensued, the Indians believing that pursuit of the marauders was useless, that the retiring Senecas might be at this time "at the head of the Patapscoe river," and could not be overtaken, yet they consented "To assist as Pilates and to joyne in the pursuite ag^t the Seneeaes," and the next morning they were promptly at the place appointed for meeting for that purpose. They were then again taxed as being themselves the authors of the injuries complained of, "and they vtterly denyed the Same and showed an old Paper and a Meddall wth a black and Yellow Ribbond thereto and the Said Indians did say that the Same was a pleadge of peace given and left with them by the former Governors as a Token of Amity and friendship as long as the Sun and Moone should last." Major Truman declared to them that he "did believe the Senecaes had done the Mischeife and not they and that he was well Satisfied Therein;" yet he placed six Indians under guard and consulted with the Virginia officers, as the affidavit expresses it

"Sitting upon a Tree Some distance from the Indians and after Some While they all Rose and came towards the Judians and Caused them to be Bound, and after Some time they talked againe (the Virginians and particularly Collon^n Wasshington urging the most sanguinary course) soe after further discourse the s^d Indians were carryed forth from the place where they were bound & they knocked them on the head" (2 Ar. 476, 483).

So utterly inexcusable was the act that the Lower House of the General Assembly accused Major Truman of murder;—the Upper House investigated it, examined witnesses, and the Major himself, who made no denial of the allegations against him. He was adjudged guilty and thereupon the Lower House sent the Upper House a bill of attainder against him to which the answer returned was. that " His Lop and this House doe Conceave it not Safe for them To Vote the killing of Susquehannoughs Embassadors noe Murther for to them and all the world it does and will Certainely appear the greatest that ever hath been Committed " (2 Ar. 503). And the Upper House informed the Lower " That this house Cannot Consent to inflict a pecuniary punishment upon a person who hath been accused by the Lower House of Murder and by this House found guiltie of the Same " (Id. 512). As the result of this disagreement, as to the *mode* of punishment, between the two houses no punishment at all was inflicted upon Major Truman. In fact it may be doubted whether there was any very earnest desire for his punishment. It was only Indians that he had killed, and though the manner in which it was done was not to be commended, the thing done was not to be too severely condemned. The destruction of wolves was encouraged by the payment of a bounty from the colonial treasury (1 Ar. 346, 362, 372, 428, 446 ; 2 Ar. 325, 348, &c.), that of the Indians, as we have seen in repeated instances, by granting to any who would take it, the "pillage," the "spoile" of them, and the prisoners themselves for servants. This record of their treatment of the aborigines is probably the darkest chapter in the history of the colonists.

In the journal of 1666 "articles of peace and amity " between the Lord Proprietary and the

"Indians of Pascataway Anacostanck Doags" and eight other tribes are recorded, and in these the device of Indian reservations first appears. This treaty is one of the most liberal towards the Indians of any that were negotiated, for it expressly provides that "the privilidge of hunting Crabbing fishing & fowleing shall be preserved to the Indians inviolably;" but the sort of equality recognized appears from a comparison of the fourth article, which reads "If an Indian kill an Englishman he shall dye for itt," with the eighth article which reads "John Roberts & Thomas Morris shall pay the Indians of Chingwawatcick one hundred and twenty armes length of Roaneoake for the Indian that was slayne by them at the head of Portoback Creeke in August last." This unusual severity for the killing of that Indian was probably owing to the fact that at this time the "Queene of Portoback" was under the special protection of the Lord Proprietary. Three years before she had made a piteous complaint of the trespasses and injuries done her by the colonists, and the Lieutenant General had issued a proclamation forbidding the colonists to seat any land within three miles of her "habitacōns or plantacōns" (3 Ar. 489).

The treaty with the several tribes above named "declares the sole pwer of Constituting and appoynting the Emperor of Pascatoway to be &

remayne in the R^t Hono^{ble} Caecilius Lord and Prop^r of this Province & his heirs;" (this right had been asserted several years previously) (3 Ar. 454, 482). It appoints a king for the "Indians of Hangemaick" and it provides "that the severall nacōns afores^d shall continue vpon the places where they now live," the bounds of these places to be fixed by the Governor "as to him in justice shall seeme most for the publick good" "within which bounds it shall not be lawfull for the s^d nacōns to entertayne any forreign Indians whatsoever to liue with them" (2 Ar. 25, 26).

Similar steps were taken for the "proteccon" of the Indians of the Easterne Shoare near Choptank" in 1669 (Id. 197, 200), and for the "Mattapany & Patuxon Indians in 1674" (Id. 354, 360, 369, 373).

A treaty of inviolable peace and perpetual amity and friendship had been "established and confirmed with several of the tribes of the "Easterne Shoare" in July, 1659 (3 Ar. 363).

In February, 1675, "some of the greate men of the Sussquehannoughs" appeared in the General Assembly and "desired to Know what part of the Province should for the future be allotted to them to Occupy." The Governor was left "to appointe a place;" the Assembly "seeing nothing for it to doe but to provide armes Ammunition and Provision, and imediately to beginne the warre" (2

Ar. 451), and they passed "an act for the Raysing a present Supply (50,000 pounds of tobacco) for his Excellency the Capt. Generall to defray the Charges of making Peace with the Cynegoe Indians and making warr with the Susquehannes Indians" (Id. 462). How Major Truman conducted that war we have already seen.

Other treaties (so-called) bound the Indians more rigidly to their good behavior. That with the Passayoncke Indians in 1661 provided "that in case any Englishman for the future shall happen to finde any Passayoncke Indian Killing either Cattle or Hoggs that then it shall be lawfull for the English to kill the said Indian" (3 Ar. 433), and that with the "Delaware Bay Jndians," in 1663, contained precisely the same provision (Id. 486).

Religion.

Probably nothing in the early history of Maryland possesses more interest, and certainly nothing requires more care and delicacy in the handling than the question of the religion of the colonists. Hallam, speaking of this era in England, says "religion was the fashion of the age," and it is evident that when the colonists crossed the ocean they did not leave this fashion behind them. No characteristic is more prominent in all their language than religious phrase which abounds in acts of Assembly, proclamations, commissions, and so forth to a degree that seems to us to savor of irreverence, if not of blasphemy. Proclamations issued even upon unimportant subjects commenced "To all persons to whom these presents shall come Greeting in the name of our Lord God everlasting," and oaths, used on any and all occasions, commonly concluding "So help you God and by the contents of this booke" (3 Ar. 193, 197, 214, 218, &c.), were so multiplied, that the General Assembly at length interposed its humble request to the Proprietary "that such things as your Lordship may hereafter desire of us may be done with as little Swearing as Conveniently may be Experience teaching us that a great Occasion is given to much perjury when swearing becometh common" (1 Ar. 242). Lord Baltimore, if requiring less religion of his subordinates than the Puritans of New England, yet required at least high moral if not religious character of them. In his full letter of instructions to Governor Stone in 1651, he ordered that no person should be "of our Council of State Commander of a County or Justice of the Peace" who lived "scandalously or Viciously with any Lewd Woman or professed himself of no religion or was an usual Drunkard Swearer or Curser" (1 Ar. 333); and the same principle that has remained undisturbed to the present time was adopted in 1654, under the commissioners of the

Commonwealth, when it was enacted that "Noe work shall be done on the Sabboth day but that which is of Necessity and Charity to be done no Inordinate Recreations as fowling fishing hunting or other, no shouting of gunns to be used on that day except in Case of Necessity" (1 Ar. 343). This was a change from four years earlier when the journal of a sitting of the Assembly is dated "April 6th 1650 Sabbath" (1 Ar. 261). When this Sabbath law was passed it was apparently supposed that the business of ordinary keepers fell within the category of necessity or charity, but it was subsequently determined that it was a "Prophanacōn of the Sabbath or Lords Day" to sell strong liquors or permit "tippling or gaming att Cards dice, ninepinn playing or other such unlawfull exercises," and the same was expressly prohibited, under the penalty of two thousand pounds of tobacco, and other disabilities (2 Ar. 414).

It cannot be expected that the Archives will end the controversy so long and earnestly contested as to who is entitled to the credit of the much-vaunted religious liberty of the colony. But there are a few facts which clearly appear: first, that the sovereign who granted the charter was not a Roman Catholic, nor was that the religion of the State at the time: Second, that Lord Baltimore, to whom the charter was granted, was a Roman Catholic: and Third, that the colonists were mingled,

Roman Catholic and Protestant; all deeply imbued with the religious sentiment of the age, zealous for their own creed, and desirous, by appeals to prejudice as well as to reason, of giving their own as far as practicable an advantage over the opposite, which they *knew* was heresy, yet prepared under the circumstances surrounding them to give for the time being, a qualified toleration to such heresy, though neither of the parties was free from the bigotry of the age, or had any clear perception of equal religious liberty and right, or of a religion neither dominating the civil government nor dominated by the civil government.

It is also clear that the controlling influence, at first, was one that had great regard for the recognized Christian Saints. A large portion of the places to which the settlers gave names bear the names of some of the saints of the calendar, and later the names are strongly suggestive of Puritan origin. Thus we find the Council assembled in June, 1662, at a place named "The Resurrection," and ordering that "a pryson bee built there" (3 Ar. 460); and when the Protestants made a home upon the Severn they named it "Providence" (1 Ar. 260), and though an act of Assembly erected it into a County by the name of "Annarundell County" (Id. 292), another act, four years later (1654), "Declared that the County now Called 'Annarundell County' shall be Called and Recorded by the name of the County of Providence" (Id. 345). The same spirit that insisted upon that name was willing to dismiss the "St." from names already given, and we find "St. Maries County" is changed in use (1654) into "maryes County" or "County of Maryes" (Id. 340, 354). We find also the early dates fixed by Saints' days. The General Assembly is to convene on the "morrow after the feast of St. Simon and St. Jude" (1 Ar. 113), on "Monday after St. James' Day" (Id. 127), "at the two most usual feasts of the year vizt the Annunciation of the Blessed Virgin Mary and Saint Michael the Arch Angell" (3 Ar. 234), "at the ffeast of our Lords nativity" (Id. 267), &c.

As religion was the great matter of contest in England, so it entered in no slight degree into the affairs of the colony from the first. When Lord Baltimore (George Calvert), in 1629, driven by snow and ice from the inhospitable shores of Avalon, went prospecting to Virginia, Governor Potts and the Virginia Council remonstrated with the home government against granting him any special privileges, because he and his followers made "profession of the Romishe Religion" and they say that:

"amonge the many blessings and favores for which wee are bound to bless God and which this Colony hath receaved from his most gracious Majesty, there is none whereby it hath beene made more happy then in the freedom of *our* Religion which we have enjoyed and that noe papists have been suffered to settle their abodes amongst us" (3 Ar. 17).

But the remonstrance was ineffectual. The Lord at home was more influential than the colonists across the sea; and when, about three years later (1632), the charter was granted to Lord Baltimore (Caecilius), the reason assigned was because he was "moved by a certain laudable and pious zeal for extending the Christian religion and extending our empire in parts of America hitherto uncultivated and inhibited by Savages and knowing nothing of the Divine Being" (3 Ar. 3). Strangely enough for the times there was granted to him, though of a different creed from the sovereign and the State, "the patronages and advowsons of all Churches which (with the increasing worship and religion of Christ) shall be built, together with license and faculty of erecting and founding Churches, Chapels and places of Worship and of causing the same to be dedicated and consecrated according to the Ecclesiastical Laws of our Kingdom of England" (Id. 4).

As soon as legislation began religion began to be nursed. In the session of 1638–9, when everything important was considered and nothing enacted, among the bills that reached the point of engrossment, was one that "Holy Church within this Province shall have all her rights liberties and immunities safe whole and inviolable in all things" (1 Ar. 35, 40, 83). The next year it fared better, and was enacted that "Holy Church within this Province shall have and enjoy all her Rights liberties and Franchises wholy and without Blemish" (Id. 96). Another bill in that session of 1638-9 made "eating flesh in time of Lent or on other days when it is prohibited by the Law of England" a crime punishable by a fine of five pounds of tobacco (Id. 53), but "idolatry which is the worshipping a false God or to commit blasphemy which is accursing or wicked speaking of God was a felony to be punished by hanging" (Id. 71). The use of proper language was further sought to be secured by enactments that "every one convicted of prophane cursing and Swearing shall forfeit five ł Tob." (Id. 159, 193).

In March, 1641, there "was presented by David Wickliffe in the name of the Protestant Catholics of Maryland" a petition, and complaint of the obstruction of Protestant worship, and Thomas Gerard, against whom this "petition of the Protestants" was directed, on hearing by the Assembly, was found "guilty of a misdemeanor" and fined "500 ł tobacco towds the maintenance of the first minister as should arrive" (1 Ar. 119).

The journal of the English House of Lords shows that on the 28th of November, 1645, there was presented to "the Com^{tee} of Lords & Comons for fforraigne Plantacōns The Peticōn of diuerse the Inhabitants of Maryland setting forth the tyranicall Gouernement of that Province, euer since its first settling, by Recusants; whoe haue seduced and forced many of his Ma^{ty} Subiects, from their Religion," and humbly praying the assistance and protection of the Parliament. " Diuers marchants of the Citty of London trading to the English plantations," also petitioned to the same effect, because, they said, " the said Lord Baltimore and his agents have not only acted horridd things in that province as Papists and Enemyes, but alsoe tearmes the Hono^{bl} Parlyament Rebells " (Id. 181). Undoubtedly the hand of Ingle was in these petitions, yet on consideration of them it was (December 25th, 1645) "Ordered by the Lords in Parlyament assembled, That the Comittee for foraigne Plantations, doe drawe vp an Ordinance and present it to this House for the settling of the Plantation of Maryland vnder the Comand of Protestants " (3 Ar. 164–5). The committee presented an ordinance accordingly, ordaining and declaring "that the said Cecil Caluert Lord of Baltimore hath wickedly broken the trust reposed in him by the said Lres Patents, and that it is convenient and necessary that the said Lres Patents bee repealed and made voyde," and that there be appointed "an able Governor and fitt Officers of the Protestant Religion and well affected to the Parlyament" (3 Ar. 173). All that followed under this ordinance these Archives do not disclose. They do show, however, that the Governorship of the colony passed, for the time being, out of the Calvert family, and that William Stone, a Protestant, became Governor. In his official oath he swore, among other things, "I will not by myself nor any Person directly or indirectly trouble molest or discountenance any Person whatsoever in the said Province professing to believe in Jesus Christ and in particular no Roman Catholick for or in respect of his or her Religion nor in his or her free exercise thereof" (3 Ar. 210). Precisely the same provision was inserted in the oath of the councillors, a majority of whom were Protestants (Id. 214).

From other sources we know that the three following were very busy years in England, and the climax was reached on the thirtieth of January, 1649, when the king lost his life upon the scaffold, and Oliver Cromwell became protector of the Commonwealth.

Three months after the king's death on the twenty-first of April, 1649, the General Assembly at St. Maries passed "AN ACT CONCERNING RELIGION," which sixteen months later (August 26th, 1650), was "confirmed by the Lord Proprietary under his hand and seale" (1 Ar. 244).

It becomes us, as loyal Marylanders, not to smile when we hear this famous statute called "an act of toleration," and to forget, if we can, that the great bulk of it is composed of penalties—fines, whippings, severe whippings, banishment, confiscation and death, against all sorts and forms of errors and heresies save those held by the persons enacting it, and to remember only that it contains the famous and familiar toleration clause; that if we except the enormous exception which it contains, it embodies a declaration of religious liberty as broad and full as can be found in any nation or language—a veritable jewel in a toad's head. But putting the worst construction upon this as a penal act, it certainly gave a larger freedom (or at least a different freedom), than was agreeable to the authorities in England. Among the instructions to the Commissioners for "reducing the colonies to their due obedience to the Commonwealth of England" was one to see that the act of Parliament "for abollishing the booke of common prayer was received and enforced" (3 Ar. 265). And Cromwell, in his tender care for their religious welfare, wrote them a letter from Whitehall, in January, 1653, in which he advised "That Love be cherished and the great Interest of Religion be owned and countenanced whereby you will ingage God's care over you, who alone can make your affairs prosperous," &c. (3 Ar. 297). And the next year it was "Enacted and declared in the Name of his Highness the Lord Protector and by the

Authority of the Generall Assembly That none who profess and exercise the Popish Religion Commonly known by the Name of the Roman Catholick Religion can be protected in this Province by the Lawes of England . . but such as profess faith in God by Jesus Christ (though differing in Judgment from the Doctrine and Discipline Publickly held forth shall not be restrained from, but shall be protected in the Profession of the faith) & Exercise of their Religion . . provided that this liberty be not extended to Popery or Prelacy," &c. (1 Ar. 341). The commissioners for settling the affairs of the Province had previously declared that all such as "doe profess the Roman Catholick Religion" should be disabled to sit in the General Assembly (3 Ar. 313).

In 1656 Lord Baltimore by proclamation (3 Ar. 325), declares the "act whereby all persons who profess to believe in Jesus Christ have liberty of conscience and free Exercise of theyr religion" is to be duly observed; and in 1657 he "doth Faithfully promise vpon his Honor to obserue and performe as much as in him lyes" the said act (Id. 334), and re-guarantees the same in 1659 (Id. 384).

Religious solicitude for the young appeared in 1671, when there was proposed "an act for the founding and Erecting of a School or College within this Province for the Education of youth in learning and Virtue," one of the provisions of which was "That the Tutors or School Masters of the said School or College may be qualified according to the reformed Church of England or that there may be two School Masters, the One for the Catholick and the Other for the Protestants Children and that the Protestants may have liberty to Choose their School Master" (2 Ar. 262-4). And in the same spirit the Upper house, at the same session, desired to have incorporated in the "act for the Preservation of Orphan's Estates," a provision that "First Care must be taken to have the Children Educated in the Religion of their dec^d Parents" (2 Ar. 317). But disagreement as to the details of the project for a school or college caused it to fail entirely; both parties apparently preferring that the youth should grow up without either "learning or Virtue," than that they should have learning and virtue of a different brand from their own.

Quakers.

Of course there might be errors and heresies so great as to give serious cause of alarm and call for the most rigorous action. Such an one was discovered by the colonial Council in 1658 in "the increase of Quakers whos denyall of subscribing the engagement," in addition to the threatening attitude of the Indians, gave such "cause of jealousies" that Captain John Odber was commissioned to put the militia at once on a war footing; and it being discovered that Thomas Thurston and Josias Cole had remained in the Province above a month without taking the oath of fidelity, it was "Ordered That a Warrant should jssue for the apprehension of said Thurston and Cole to answer theyr misdemeanors" (3 Ar. 348). The warrant was issued "to the sheriffe of Annarundell to take the body of Josias Cole and him in safe custody keepe vt in order without Baile or Mainprise" (Id. 350). And an order went "to the Sheriffe of Caluert County to bring the body of Thomas Thurston to Mr. Henry Coursey's by the twenty-fifth of July." These orders were executed and then the council discovered the magnitude of their undertaking, for not only had they Thurston and Cole on their hands, but they were compelled to take

"into consideracōn the insolent behaviour of som people called Quakers who at the Court in contempt of an order then made & proclaimed would presumptiously stand covered and not only so, but also refuse to subscribe the engagement in that case provided alleadging they were to be governed by Gods lawe and the light within them and not by mans lawe and vpon full debate . . . ordered that all persons should take & subscribe the said engagement by the 20th of August next or else depart the Province by the 25th of March followeing vpon paine due to Rebbells & Traitors" (3 Ar. 352), and the Governor issued his proclamation accordingly. Even this did not rescue the province from the great danger of Quakers, and the next July the Council

"Ordered as followeth : viz Whereas it is to well knowne in this Province that there haue of late bin seuerall vagabonds & Jdle persons knowne by the name of Quakers that haue presumed to com into this Province as well diswading the People from Complying with the Military discipline in this time of Danger as also from giuing testimony or being Jurors in causes depending betweene party & party or bearing any office in the Province to the no small disturbance of the Lawes & Civill Govern^t thereof: And that the keeping & detayning them as Prisoners hath brought so great a charge vpon this Province the Governor & Councell taking it into theyr Consideracon haue thought fitt to Appoint & doe hereby for the prevention of the like inconveniences for the time to com Require & command all & euery the Justices of the Peace of this Province that so soone as they shall haue notice that any of the foresaid Vagabonds or Jdle persons shall againe presume to com into this Province they forthwith cause them to be apprehended & whipped from Constable to Constable vntill they be sent out of the Province" (3 Ar. 362).

Thurston, who still remained, was arrested under this order, but succeeded with much adroitness in showing that it did not apply to his case, whereupon, determined that if the general order did not cover his case, a special order should be made that would, the Council ordered as follows:

"The board doth Judge That the said Thurston be for euer bannished this Province & that if he be found within this Province at any time 7 days after the date heereof or shall att any time after returne againe into this Province that he be by the next Justice of the Peace caused to be whipt with 30 lashes & so sent from Constable to Constable till he be Conveyed out of the Province. And that if he shall then at any time againe presume to returne into this Province that he be whipt with 30 lashes at euery Constables & be againe sent out of the Province as aforesaid. And it is further ordered that no person whatsoeuer presume to receaue harbour or conceale the said Thomas Thurston after the tenth day of this Present month vpon Paine of fiue hundred pounds of Tob for euery time that they shall so Receaue harbour or Conceale him the said Thomas Thurston" (3 Ar. 364).

Those, who, for conscience sake, refused to bear arms, were proceeded against by court martial, though these Archives do not show precisely what penalty was inflicted upon them (3 Ar. 435, 441, 456). Their meetings to confer over their persecutions were thought to be full of danger to the colony (Id. 494–5), so that in 1666 the Council "Ordered that the Secretary doe forthwith issue out warr^{ts} to each respective sheriffe for the taking the names of such persons within their Balywick who goes und^r the Notion of Quakers and to make return in a list of theire names and surnames at the next Prouin^{all} Court" (Id. 547).

But they were not all driven away from the Province, or into concealment. In 1674 Wenlock

Chriterson, well known in history for his courage and steadfastness in maintaining the principles and practices of his sect in Boston, having found a fresh field in Talbot County, with others "of us who are in Scorne called Quakers," sent a petition to the General Assembly to be allowed to discharge certain duties, especially those of witnesses and administrators without taking an oath (2 Ar. 355). This difficult question gave the Assembly much and painful deliberation, but after two years the Lower House announced its conclusion, that, "this house doe Conceave it utterly unsafe for the Ld Propriet^y to make any Law in this Province to exempt the people called Quakers from testifying vpon Oath and therefore thinke it Unfitt for this house to advise his Lords^p to Condescend to any votes of either house of assembly tending that way" (2 Ar. 492).

Temperance.

Among the perplexing questions with which the colonists were called to deal, was one which has not yet entirely lost its interest, nor as to the best manner of dealing with which is there yet entire unanimity. Legislation on the subject was largely experimental then, it is hardly other than that now. Among the very first bills brought before the General Assembly of the Province was one

"For restraint of Liquors" (1 Ar. 34); and in the "act for the authority of Justices of the Peace," at the same session, it was provided that for "Drunkenness which is Drinking with excess to the notable perturbation of any organ of sence or motion the offender shall forfeit to the Lord Proprietary thirty pound of tobacco or five Shillings Sterling, or otherwise shall be whipped or by some other Corporall Shame or punishment Corrected for every such excess at the discretion of the judge" (1 Ar. 53).

Pursuing the same policy, that is, treating drinking itself as the crime, the General Assembly, in 1642, enacted that "every one convicted of being drunk shall forfeit 100 ℔ tobacco toward the building of a prison . . or if the offender be a Servant and have not wherewith to Satisfie the fine he shall be imprisoned or sett in the Stocks or bilbos fasting for twenty-four hours" (1 Ar. 159, 193). Substantially the same was the act of 1650 (Id. 286). The act of 1654 went further and made it the duty of "every officer and Magistrate in the Province from the highest to the Lowest to use all Lawfull meanes to convict such as to their knowledge shall be Drunke;" and it imposed an equal fine upon "every person in this Province that shall see anyone Drunk and shall not within three days make it known to the next Magistrate" (Id. 342). The "act concerning Drunkness" of 1658 provided a severer penalty, and enacted "that hee that shalbe lawfully convicted of drunkeness shall for the first offense be sett in the Stocks Six houres, or pay one hundred pounds of tobacco, ffor the second offense to be publickly whipt or pay three hundred pounds of Tobacco. Being the third tyme convicted as aforesaid, the Offender shalbe adiudged a Person infamous, and thereby made vncapable of giving vote, or bearing Office within this Province during the space of three years next after such Conviction" (Id. 375).

The "Vpper howse" of the General Assembly itself imposed this penalty upon Thomas Hills, and for "sweareing" when in his cups, compelled him to "goe to the lower howse and there accknowledge his faults with expressing his hearty sorrow for the same" (Id. 404). But if the culprit was an official he did not escape so easily. Thomas Gerard was a member of the Council, and against him his "Lordships attorney generall" filed an information in 1658, charging that he, "to the Greate offense of Almighty God dishonor of his Lordship & whole Counccll hath diverse times misbehaued himselfe & offended in Drunkennes & other Lewd behaviour Committed on board of Covills ship Rideing in St. Georges River," &c. With the information were filed certain affidavits evidently designed to screen him as far as the facts would permit. Mr. Henry Coursey swore "that he was on board of Covills ship with Mr. Gerrard that the said Gerrard had drunke something extraordinary but was not so much in drinke but he could gett out of a Carts way" (3 Ar. 354). Upon this information, for his "crimes and misdemeanors," he was banished from the Province with "forfeiture and Conficacōn of all his estate both reall and personall;" and though the Governor afterwards remitted that sentence, so far as banishment was concerned, yet it was permitted to stand as a forfeiture of all franchises and he was required to "give Recognizance for his Good behaviour" (Id. 409).

Besides treating drunkenness as a crime in the drinker, some effort was made to discourage too loose a traffic in spirits. The act of 1638-9 provided that where the goods of or in the hands of any person are not sufficient to pay all his debts . . debts for wine and hot waters shall not be Satisfied till all other debts be paid" (1 Ar. 84).

A strong effort was made in 1674 to impose a heavy duty upon liquors imported, and both houses voted a prohibition of their importation from New England, New Yorke, and Virginia, yet the vote does not seem to have been matured into law (2 Ar. 361, 375 to 380). They recognized the necessity of taverns in a country like theirs, but they recognized also the importance of having good citizens only for inn-keepers, and sent a message to his Excellency to request that he would issue "a license to keep Ordinary to noe person but th^t he shall give Bond to his Excellency with good Sureties that they shall Suffer noe drinking or gameing upon the Sabboth day," &c. (2 Ar. 346); and by another act liquor selling on the Sabbath was strictly prohibited (Id. 414). But to them an ordinary without liquors was the play of Hamlet with Hamlet's part left out. A license for an ordinary was a license "to keep an Inn or Ordinary And to make Sale of Beer wine Strong Waters or any other fitting and wholesome Drink Vittualls or provisions" (3 Ar. 304). But the Inn-keepers must have been very rapacious, for act after act was passed, fixing the prices which they might charge for each liquor which they furnished in a list long enough to shame the wine card of fashionable hotels of the present day. These lists include French Brandy, French wine, Canary, Malligoe, Madeira, Fayal, "Portoport and other Portugall wine," strong Cider, "Clarrett," "Strong Beere or Ale," "Rumm," English Spirits, "dutch dramms," "Annisseed Rosa Solis," Perry, Quince, Lime Juice, Rhenish wines, Sherry, Mumm and various others (2 Ar. 148, 214, 296). But they voted that "no ordinary keeper within this Province shall at any time charge anything to Account for Bowles of punch or any quantity of mixed Drink but shall only sell the several Ingredients to the said mixture" at the rates they had prescribed (Id. 268). The Inn-keepers of course found it no difficult task to fix their liquors to suit the prices fixed on them by the Assembly, which soon led the Assembly to "Conceave th^t the underrating of the s^d Liquors hath been the Occasion of the Sophisticacōn of Liquors" and therefore "Voted by this house th^t noe rates or prices of anie Accomodacōns be set or Ascertained but of such only as are of absolute necessity for Sustaining & Refreshing of Travellers (th^t is to say) Horse meate mans meate Small Beare & Lodging" (2 Ar. 351, 407, 560). But they were at their wit's end in their effort to find the proper limit to ordinaries, that is, to fix the point which would supply the necessities of travellers, and would not promote dissipation in the youth or in the homes of the colonists. It was plain to see that there must be an ordinary where the General Assembly met, and where the Courts were held; and there many wished the licenses to stop. But after much deliberation it was agreed to request the Governor "by proclamation to suppress all other Ordinaries in this Province but that where the Provinciall Court & County Courts are kept and Besides in Ann Arundell County at Richard Hills, in Patuxent at Richard Keenes & George Beckwiths, in Dorchester County at Peter Underwoods and one at the Wading Place between Kent and Talbot

Counties and no more in the whole Province" (2 Ar. 432, 4). This was in 1675, and a complete reversal of the policy which they pursued in 1662, when "for the better Encouragement of all honest and well minded people whoe now doe or which shall hereafter Keepe Victualling howses" they conferred upon them special authority and power substantially equivalent to that enjoyed by a landlord in the matter of distraining for rent (1 Ar. 447).

To them a State House without an ordinary as an attachment was an absurdity, if not an impossibility. When they framed "an act for the purchaseing a State howse" at St. Maries for 12,000 pounds of tobacco, they stipulated that the vendor, Mrs. Hannah Lee, should "dwell and keep ordinary in the same for the tearme of three yeers" (1 Ar. 447, 455); and when later they engaged William Smith "to repaire the Cuntry's howse at St. Mary's, he was bound to keep ordinary therein for seauen years" (1 Ar. 538; 2 Ar. 50, 51), but they did not mean that he should impose upon the colony any exorbitant charge for the entertainment of its officials, and as they scrutinized his bill in 1666 they decided

"vppon debate This Howse is willing to allow Will[m] Smyth his acc[t] w[ch] hee hath charged the burgesses this Assembly for Liquors: As wine, rumme, Brandy Punch & Liminade made with Wine. But th[t] w[ch] hee calls

Liminade wthout strong drinke they will allow only 25 1 pr gallon, And as to their dyett & Lodging they will allow what they iustly may be charged withall & noe more" (2 Ar. 127).

The same frugal mind in the matter of spirits was in the Council when they laid in their supplies for the military expedition against the Eastern Shore Indians in May, 1639, for they at that time provided for the soldiers of the expedition a whole barrel of oatmeal, but only "4 cases of hot waters" (3 Ar. 85, see also Id. 345).

ATTORNEYS.

Besides the Indians and Quakers there was another class of men which fell under the suspicion of at least a portion of the colonists and which, incredible as it seems to us they felt that they needed some protection against. This appears first from the report of a joint committee of the General Assembly in 1669, in which the "real grievances of the Province" are set forth. The fourth specification of these grievances says: "That the Privileged Attorneys are one of the Grand Grievances of the Country." At the same time Robert Morris went before the lower house of Assembly, and there did "in the name of the Commons of this Province impeach Mr John Morecroft Gen^t being one of the Attorneys of the

Provincial Court for exacting fees above and beyond the Laws & Customs of this Province & that he is retayned as attorney for some with unreasonable fees, for a whole year's space so that by that means it Causes several Suits to the Utter Ruin of people" (2 Ar. 167).

Five years later there was passed "An Act to reforme the attorneys counsellors & Solicit[rs] at law of this Province to avoyde unnecessary Suites and Charges att Law" (Id. 409). From the character and reputation which that class of people have borne from that time to the present, we are forced to conclude, either that the grievance complained of was rather fancied than real, or else that the reform which was enacted was completely successful, and has been permanent.

WITCHCRAFT.

There was another class of people quite as objectionable to the colonists as Quakers and Attorneys, and, if possible, more difficult to deal with. This was the witches, against whom the capital statute of James was invoked, and at least in the case of Mary Lee, on her way to the colony, execution was had by the same law (Lynch law) by which one Cooper was recently executed in Baltimore County. The particulars of this execution are given in two affidavits made before and filed with the Council in

June, 1654. The story as told by one of the deponents, Henry Corbyn, of London, merchant,

"Saith That at Sea upon his this Deponents Voyage hither in the Ship called the Charity of London m^r John Bosworth being Master and about a fortnight or three weeks before the said Ships arrivall in this Province of Maryland, or before a Rumour amongst the Seamen was very frequent, that one Mary Lee then aboard the said Ship was a witch, the Said Seamen Confidently affirming the Same upon her own deportment and discourse, and then more Earnestly then before Importuned the Said Master that a tryall might be had of her which he the Said Master m^r Bosworth refused, but resolved (as he expressed to put her ashore upon the Barmudoes) but Cross wids p^{r}vented and the Ship grew daily more Leaky almost to desperation and the Chiefe Seamen often declared their Resolution of Leaving her if an opportunity offerred it Self which aforesaid Reasons put the Master upon a Consultation with m^r Chipsham and this deponent, and it was thought fitt, Considering our Said Condition to Satisfie the Seamen, in a way of trying her according to the Usuall Custome in that kind whether she were a witch or Not and Endeavoured by way of delay to have the Commanders of other Ships aboard but Stormy weather prevented, In the Interime two of the Seamen apprehended her without order and Searched her and found Some Signall or Marke of a witch upon her, and then calling the Master m^r Chipsham and this Deponent with others to See it afterwards made her fast to the Capstall betwixt decks, And in the morning the Signall was Shrunk into her body for the Most part, And an Examination was thereupon importuned by the Seamen which this deponent was desired to take whereupon She Confessed as by her Confession appeareth, and upon that the Seamen Importuned the Said Master to put her to Death (which as it Seemed he was unwilling to doe, and went into his Cabbinn, but being more Vehemently pressed to it he tould them they might do what they would and went into his Cabbinn, and Sometime before they were about that Action he desired this depon' to acquaint them that they Should doe no more then what they Should Justifie which they Said they would doe by laying all their hands in generall to the Execution of her." (3 Ar. 306).

The "deposition of ffrancis Darby" fully corroborates Mr. Corbyn in all material points, but especially in showing the effort of the master of the ship to escape all responsibility for the execution.

The colonists were evidently in sympathy with the sentiment expressed by Wesley, three-quarters of a century later, that "giving up witchcraft was, in fact, giving up the Bible;" and, as we have seen in considering the criminal law, they placed it, under the name of sorcery, by the side of blasphemy and idolatry, as a capital offence, repeatedly in their statutes.

The charge to Justices and other officers, often repeated in these Archives, was "to enquire of all manner of Fellonyes witchcrafts inchantments Sorceries Magick Arts trespasses forestallings ingrossings and Extorcons whatsoeuer" (3 Ar. 422, 535, 554, &c.)

That this diligent quest was not always fruitless is shown by a "Petition of the Deputies and Delegates of the Lower House of Assembly," presented to the Governor in February, 1675. This petition humbly showed to his Excellency:

"That whereas Iohn Cowman being Arraigned Convicted and Condemned upon the statute of the first King Iames of England &c for Witchcraft Conjuration Sorcery or Enchantment used upon the Body of Elizabeth Goodale and now Lying under that Condemnation, and hath humbly Implored and Beseeched Us your Lordships Petitioners to Mediate and Intercecde in his behalf with your Excellency for a Reprieve and Stay of Execution—
Your Excellencies Petitioners do therefore accordingly in all Humble manner beseech your Excellency that the Rigour and Severaity of the Law to which the said Condemned Malefactor hath Miserably Exposed himself may be remitted and Relaxed by the Exercise of your Excellencys Mercy & Clemencie upon so wretched and Miserable an Object" (2 Ar. 425).

This petition met a gracious reception for it was answered that:

"The Lieutenant General hath Considered of the Petition here above and is willing upon the request of the Lower house that the Condemned Malefactor be reprieved and Execution Stayed, Provided that the Sheriff of St. Maries County carry him to the Gallows, and that the rope being about his neck it be there made known to him how much he is Beholding to the Lower house of Assemblie for Mediating and Interceeding in his Behalf with the Lieu^t General and that he remain at the City of St. Maries to be employed in such service as the Governor and Council shall thinke fitt during the Pleasure of the Governor" (Ibid.)

In what the Governor could safely employ one having the elusive power of a witch we can only conjecture. It may be that he desired to use him as an instrument for the punishment of other criminals, as he had precedent for doing in the action of Leonard Calvert, who, when Governor, "exchanged the sentence of death of John dandy into service for 7 yeares to his Lop & to remaine exequutioner of all corporall corrections according to the writts lawfully directed to him" (3 Ar. 146).

May we not hope that the succeeding volumes of the Archives will show that this vigilance, or this executive clemency, in dealing with witches, induced all of that class of malefactors to leave the Province, and migrate, on their broomsticks, to Salem, Massachusetts, where they had an epidemic of them some fifteen or twenty years later!

But for the contemporaneous records, presented to us in these volumes of "Archives," it would seem hardly credible that the state of things which they demonstrate, could have existed where we now live. The rude life, the stern struggle with nature and man, the liberality hampered by bigotry, the abject submission coupled with bold assertion of right, the burning religious zeal joined with forgetfulness of the charity that true religion requires, form a picture of the Spirit of the Times in which light and shadow are strangely mingled. If we find details which feed our pride, we find others that lead us back to humility; and while we regret the "good old times" we can but heartily congratulate ourselves that they have passed away. Looking back across the gulf of two hundred and fifty years, our greatest occasion of rejoicing is at the progress made—at the abundant proof furnished that "the world does move."

www.ingramcontent.com/pod-product-compliance
Lightning Source LLC
Chambersburg PA
CBHW020301090426
42735CB00009B/1169